Are You Hindered By Satan

Bible Studies, Volume 16

Leslie Rendell

Published by Leslie Rendell, 2024.

Table of Contents

Why should we study the bible? Isn't it enough to go to church once a week and listen to the Pastor?

Most Pastors who belong to one of the modern day churches have to follow what the church leaders tell them. They all have their own "statement of beliefs" to adhere too, and these doctrines vary greatly from church to church in what they see as the truth. So since they cannot all be right, then some must be wrong. What if that refers to the church you are attending, if indeed you attend any church at all. How can you know what God sees as the truth. Well, it is up to the individual to sort the wheat from the chaff. How do we do that? Only by seeking the truth that God has concealed in his book, the bible.

Consider the following passage of scripture in the book of Proverbs.

> *Pro 25:2 It is the glory of God to conceal a thing: but the honour of kings is to search out a matter.*

This is what God expects from us. We are to constantly look into the holy scriptures and find the truth that he has concealed there for us to find. Please notice that God has not concealed them from us to keep it all a secret. No, he wants us to look for the truth. This is further emphasized in the following verses from the book of Isaiah

> *Isa 28:9 Whom shall he teach knowledge? and whom shall he make to understand doctrine? them that are weaned from the milk, and drawn from the breasts.*

> *Isa 28:10 For precept must be upon precept, precept upon precept; line upon line, line upon line; here a little, and there a little:*

This backs up what we read in Proverbs 25:2, that we must search out a matter that God has concealed. This is a real treasure hunt. If we can seek the will of God in our lives, we are not rejecting him, but we are embracing him and his way of life. There is a great reward for those who are prepared to seek God with their whole hearts, read the following verse and see what this reward is.

Rom 2:7 To them who by patient continuance in well doing seek for glory and honour and immortality, eternal life:

This is why we must spend time in searching the scriptures. Looking for precept upon precept, line upon line, here a little there a little. Looking for the things God has concealed. We must search for these pearls of wisdom God has concealed in his bible.

Chapter 1 - Introduction

Writing a book about Satan is not what I really want to do. I do not want to give him any credit, praise, or worship. God, and God alone, should receive these praises. So why do I write about Satan?

Satan is a very real being and has caused and will continue to cause a great deal of pain and suffering for the entire human race. It is essential we "know our enemy", if we are going to learn how to overcome his influence upon us.

In this modern day and age, is it practical to believe in Satan, or was he relegated to history and plays no part in the affairs of the world?. This question needs to be addressed, because many people no longer believe he exists. Those who may believe he exists do not see him as any sort of threat to their welfare.

We need to understand who he is, what he has done in the past, what he is doing today, and what he plans to do in the future. He has a great deal more power than what most people are aware of. Therefore, it is vital to know as much as possible about him. Only then can we avoid the traps he sets for us.

Satan is known by several other names, such as "The Devil", or "The Evil One", or "The Prince Of The Power Of The Air". Satan is mentioned over 100 times in the Bible. This should convince us he definitely exists.

Therefore, it is imperative we know how to resist this evil spirit and the attitudes he broadcasts through the air. Fortunately for us, God has given us the knowledge we need to defeat Satan. The knowledge on how to fight him is in Eph 6:10-17.

Eph 6:10 Finally, my brethren, be strong in the Lord, and in the power of his might.

Eph 6:11 Put on the whole armour of God, that ye may be able to stand against the wiles of the devil.

Eph 6:12 For we wrestle not against flesh and blood, but against principalities, against powers, against the rulers of the darkness of this world, against spiritual wickedness in high places.

Eph 6:13 Wherefore take unto you the whole armour of God, that ye may be able to withstand in the evil day, and having done all, to stand.

Eph 6:14 Stand therefore, having your loins girt about with truth, and having on the breastplate of righteousness;

Eph 6:15 And your feet shod with the preparation of the gospel of peace;

Eph 6:16 Above all, taking the shield of faith, wherewith ye shall be able to quench all the fiery darts of the wicked.

Eph 6:17 And take the helmet of salvation, and the sword of the Spirit, which is the word of God:

These pieces of armour that we need to protect us from Satan are actually the word of God. If we learn from the bible what God expects from us, and we then do our best to live according to what we learn. Then we are putting on the full armour of God. When if we do this, we will overcome the Devil and all of his powers with the power of Almighty God.

Satan was a created angel, but because of his great beauty, he became proud and puffed up in his own eyes. There was a time when Satan lived in the very presence of God and God highly honored him. He succumbed to pride and committed great sins against God. Therefore, God cast him out of Heaven to the earth where he is present and active, even in this modern age. See how God created Satan and how he corrupted himself?

Eze 28:12 Son of man, take up a lamentation upon the king of Tyrus, and say unto him, Thus saith the Lord GOD; Thou sealest up the sum, full of wisdom, and perfect in beauty.

Eze 28:13 Thou hast been in Eden the garden of God; every precious stone was thy covering, the sardius, topaz, and the diamond, the beryl, the onyx, and the jasper, the sapphire, the emerald, and the carbuncle, and gold: the workmanship of thy tabrets and of thy pipes was prepared in thee in the day that thou wast created.

Eze 28:14 Thou art the anointed cherub that covereth; and I have set thee so: thou wast upon the holy mountain of God; thou hast walked up and down in the midst of the stones of fire.

Eze 28:15 Thou wast perfect in thy ways from the day that thou wast created, till iniquity was found in thee.

Eze 28:16 By the multitude of thy merchandise they have filled the midst of thee with violence, and thou hast sinned: therefore I will cast thee as profane out of the mountain of God: and I will destroy thee, O covering cherub, from the midst of the stones of fire.

Eze 28:17 Thine heart was lifted up because of thy beauty, thou hast corrupted thy wisdom by reason of thy brightness: I will cast thee to the ground, I will lay thee before kings, that they may behold thee.

Satan is a created being. In verse 15, God perfectly created Satan, but Satan was found to have iniquity.. This iniquity was pride. He admired his own beauty, as we see in verse 17. Therefore, because of his sins, God will destroy him when the time is right, according to God's own timetable.

Since this sinful nature was in him, he became an enemy of God and has been trying to replace God on His throne ever since.. He regards himself as superior to God, but I believe God will soon defeat him, bind him, and place him into the pit.

It is Satan's plan to be worshipped. He even had the audacity to tempt Jesus to worship him. But Jesus rebuke him with the following words. Jesus used these words to rebuke him: "You shall worship the Lord your God and serve him only," as it is written.

This pride that is a major characteristic of Satan is the opposite of our Lord's character. Jesus came as a human and was humble. Even though He had much greater power than Satan, He was content with being in appearance as a man. He humbled himself and became obedient to death, even death on a cross!". The contrast between Jesus and Satan could not be greater.

Most people who believe in Satan only see him as the devil in charge of a place called hell. But as we saw earlier, he is roaming the world looking for ways to distract us from our Saviour, Jesus Christ. This place called Hell has a very definite purpose, as we can see in

> *Mat 25:41 Then shall he say also unto them on the left hand, Depart from me, ye cursed, into everlasting fire, prepared for the devil and his angels:*

Most people usually picture Satan as a red and fiery beast in their minds. Ugly and terrifying to look at. Not the sort of figure you would want to be seen with. But Satan and his band of demons are normally portraying themselves as apostles, as leaders of churches, as this is the best way to influence members of humanity. He tries to look good so he can lead us away from the truth of God. God reveals his truth to us in.

> *2Co 11:13 For such are false apostles, deceitful workers, transforming themselves into the apostles of Christ.*

> *2Co 11:14 And no marvel; for Satan himself is transformed into an angel of light.*

> *2Co 11:15 Therefore it is no great thing if his ministers also be transformed as the ministers of righteousness; whose end shall be according to their works.*

One way Satan disguises himself is to look like an angel of light. This is not the ugly red fiery beast we may picture him as. Satan knows that the less he looks like the Devil we perceive in our minds, then the more he remains "invisible" to us. The harder it is for us to recognise him for what he is, the better he likes it.

Chapter 2 - Who is Satan

In this chapter, we will examine who Satan is and the different names he goes by.

In the book of 2Corinthians we see Satan given the title, "god of this world". What does this mean?

First, we realize that God alone is in full control of everything. From the vastness of the universe to the minuteness of the smallest particle we can see. God is in ultimate control, and Satan can only do as much as God allows him to do.

If you have any doubts about this, then may I suggest you read the "Book of Job". Here you can witness God permitting Satan to bring certain troubles to Job. But Satan could do only what God allowed.

Only one instance of the term "god of this age" appears in the entire bible. We should read and examine this passage of scripture to discover the reason behind this title being given to him..

> *2Co 4:1 Therefore, since through God's mercy we have this ministry, we do not lose heart.*

> *2Co 4:2 Rather, we have renounced secret and shameful ways; we do not use deception, nor do we distort the word of God. On the contrary, by setting forth the truth plainly we commend ourselves to everyone's conscience in the sight of God.*

> *2Co 4:3 And even if our gospel is veiled, it is veiled to those who are perishing.*

> *2Co 4:4 The god of this age has blinded the minds of unbelievers, so that they cannot see the light of the gospel that displays the glory of Christ, who is the image of God.*

> *2Co 4:5 For what we preach is not ourselves, but Jesus Christ as Lord, and ourselves as your servants for Jesus' sake.*

2Co 4:6 For God, who said, "Let light shine out of darkness," made his light shine in our hearts to give us the light of the knowledge of God's glory displayed in the face of Christ.

Who are those who are perishing in verse three above? They are certainly not innocent victims. These people's refusal to believe in Jesus Christ made it possible for Satan to blind them.

Joh 3:19 And this is the judgment: the light has come into the world, and people loved the darkness rather than the light because their works were evil.

Joh 3:20 For everyone who does wicked things hates the light and does not come to the light, lest his works should be exposed.

These men loved the darkness where they thought they could hide their evil ways. They hated the light because this allowed others to see the works they carried out. Few people realise Satan is causing "the entire world" to turn against the teaching of God and enticing them to follow the ways of the Devil. Rev 12:9 reveals this truth..

Rev 12:9 The great dragon was thrown down, the old serpent, he who is called the devil and Satan, the deceiver of the whole world. He was thrown down to the earth, and his angels were thrown down with him.

In 2Cor 4:4 above, we see it is the minds of unbelievers that Satan has veiled from the truth. But he is also actively trying to influence the heart and thoughts of people. This is another reason he is called, "The prince of the power of the air". Satan is powerful, and therefore he is called "The god of this age". However, it should be noted that "god" is spelled with a lower-case "g". He can only blind those who will not believe.

Satan is the god of this world, just the same as Baal was the god to whoever worshipped him. He is not God in the proper sense, because the earth is the LORD'S as we see in Psa 24:1.

Psa 24:1 Of David. A psalm. The earth is the LORD's, and everything in it, the world, and all who live in it;

Therefore, put your trust in the only true God of the Universe (not just the world) and worship Him only.

Telling lies is one of Satan's greatest weapons against God's chosen people. He is always using deceit to separate people from God. He uses ministers of false religions and cult leaders to spread his lies for him. Lies such as, "there is no God", "God doesn't care about you," "the Bible cannot be trusted," and one of his greatest lies is, "your good works will get you into heaven." True Christians know no amount of good works will save us.

We know Satan as the father of lies from Joh 8:44.

Joh 8:44 You are of your father, the devil, and you want to do the desires of your father. He was a murderer from the beginning, and doesn't stand in the truth, because there is no truth in him. When he speaks a lie, he speaks on his own; for he is a liar, and the father of lies.

We also see that Satan earns the reputation of being the accuser of God's people..

Rev 12:10 I heard a loud voice in heaven, saying, "Now the salvation, the power, and the Kingdom of our God, and the authority of his Christ has come; for the accuser of our brothers has been thrown down, who accuses them before our God day and night."

We can never underestimate the influence Satan has had over this world for the last approximately six thousand years.. It was he who persuaded Eve to eat from the tree of the knowledge of good and evil. Therefore, by this deception, he is responsible for the first sin against God, and for all sins ever since.

I must stress to all readers of this book, Satan is a created being. Therefore, even though he has some amazing powers, they are vastly inferior to the power of God. Refer to Eze 28:12-15 from chapter 1, to understand how Satan was created, and the beauty he possessed.. Then his fall from grace as pride of his beauty overpowered him and then his disgrace and expulsion from "The Mount of God".

The one thing we can take from this is that God has always been in complete control, still is today, and always will be.

From the time Satan is thrown out of heaven, along with his band of demons who chose to follow him, he has attempted to oppose God in everything and to lead people into rebellion against God.

One of the biggest ways he brings havoc to us is via deception. Without recognizing him as a threat, we have no reason to fear him, and we will be ignorant of the ways he brings troubles into our lives..

He is very subtle and convincing. Look at how he deceived Adam and Eve into eating from the tree of the knowledge of good and evil. Even though God had told Adam clearly that to eat of this tree was to die. But Satan told Eve that if she ate of the tree, she would not die, but would have knowledge of good and evil. Unfortunately, Eve fell for this lie, so when they allowed Satan to influence them, they disobeyed God and ever since that time mankind has suffered at the hands of Satan and the lies he has us believe.

Satan has authority over those who are in Christ, only when they give in to him and believe his lies. But we have the promise from God that Satan will be defeated, and all his evil works will be destroyed.

> *1Jn 3:8 He who sins is of the devil, for the devil has been sinning from the beginning. To this end the Son of God was revealed: that he might destroy the works of the devil.*

The words from Joh12:31 reinforce this.. Here we can see Jesus has triumphed over Satan by His sacrifice on the cross.

> *Joh 12:31 Now is the judgment of this world. Now the prince of this world will be cast out.*

It is amazing how much misinformation about our adversary comes to us from the movie theatres. This is man's imaginations, and no doubt influenced by Satan himself. Therefore, it is vital we seek the truth about him from the only reliable source of information that we can fully trust. The holy bible.

Satan has certain powers, but they are infinitely less powerful than that of our Almighty God. Jas 4:7 informs us that to defeat Satan, we must resist him by submitting ourselves to God. This verse also informs us what Satan will do if we submit ourselves to God. He will flee from us.

Jas 4:7 Be subject therefore to God. Resist the devil, and he will flee from you.

Satan will continue to influence this world with his evil ways until Jesus returns in all power and glory. When He returns, we see Satan bound with a great chain and cast into the abyss. One thing to notice here is that it is not Jesus Himself who casts Satan into the abyss. No, it is an angel of God. So we can see here that Satan's power is overcome by an angel.

Rev 20:1 I saw an angel coming down out of heaven, having the key of the abyss and a great chain in his hand.

Rev 20:2 He seized the dragon, the old serpent, which is the devil and Satan, who deceives the whole inhabited earth, and bound him for a thousand years,

Rev 20:3 and cast him into the abyss, and shut it, and sealed it over him, that he should deceive the nations no more, until the thousand years were finished. After this, he must be freed for a short time.

Satan has always been active in the world, trying to influence us to sin and to draw us away from God. One of his names is "The Prince Of The Power Of The Air". And just like we can hear things sent out on radio waves. Satan can broadcast his attitude to anyone who is vulnerable to his thoughts, because they do not have God in their lives, The Devil is "Prince of the power of the air" and those he influence are the disobedient as we can see in Eph 2:2.

Eph 2:2 in which you once walked according to the course of this world, according to the prince of the power of the air, the spirit who now works in the children of disobedience;

These disobedient are being influenced by Satan to carry out his wishes and to commit every sin possible.

We must put on the full armour of God that will protect us from Satan. This armour is the knowledge of God that we can only get from his written word, the bible.

We must learn all we can about our God and how He wants us to live. Overcome the powers of the Devil with the powers of Almighty God. The more we study God's holy scriptures, the stronger our faith will become, and it is our faith that will give us the victory over Satan.

1Jn 5:4 for everyone born of God overcomes the world. This is the victory that has overcome the world, even our faith.

In the book of 1 Peter, we receive instructions on how to defeat Satan. We are told it will not be easy and we may have to suffer for a short time. But this suffering is not something new, and Most Christians will experience it during their lives.

1Pe 5:6 Humble yourselves, therefore, under God's mighty hand, that he may lift you up in due time.

1Pe 5:7 Cast all your anxiety on him because he cares for you.

1Pe 5:8 Be alert and of sober mind. Your enemy the devil prowls around like a roaring lion looking for someone to devour.

1Pe 5:9 Resist him, standing firm in the faith, because you know that the family of believers throughout the world is undergoing the same kind of sufferings.

1Pe 5:10 And the God of all grace, who called you to his eternal glory in Christ, after you have suffered a little while, will himself restore you and make you strong, firm and steadfast.

1Pe 5:11 To him be the power for ever and ever. Amen.

All sin has its origins in Satan, as we saw earlier in.

> *1Jn 3:8 The one who does what is sinful is of the devil, because the devil has been sinning from the beginning. The reason the Son of God appeared was to destroy the devil's work.*

True Christians who are prepared to read and study their Bibles know Satan has a lot of influence over this world, and he is making things as difficult as possible for those who follow Christ.

There are many fictional characters in the world, some presumably that do good deeds like Superman, Wonder Woman, and Spider Man. Then there are the villains of the peace, such as The Penguin, The Joker and Lex Luthor. Some people around the world base their lives around these make believe characters, and even though they know they are not genuine characters, their heroes still influence them.

The sad thing is, that we have Satan, The father of all lies, who most people in the world (adults included and maybe even especially) do not believe he exists, or if they believe he exists, that he has no influence over their lives.

They do not see him as a threat, and he rarely enters their thoughts. If they believe in him, he is just a figure that dwells in a place called hell and is the main furnace stoker, and just waiting for God to send down anyone who dares to sin against Him. Unfortunately, that would be all of us!!

To believe this lie is to completely under estimate who Satan is, also known as Lucifer or the Devil. This lie is one that he is happy with because it is one of the most successful of Satan's tactics is to keep himself as invisible as possible. The fewer people who believe that he exists, the better that he likes it. When people underestimate, ignore, or deny his existence, he can inflict more damage upon the people God created in His image..

If we are not aware of his presence and tactics, then we may feel that we are in no need to protect ourselves from this unknown enemy. But he is a very real being and is also powerful. He can, and does, cause us a great deal of trouble and pain and goes to great lengths to lead us away from the truth and the proper knowledge and understanding of God.

Satan's ultimate plan is to destroy God, all of His ways, and eventually be like God himself. We can read about his ambitions in Isaiah 14 and verses 12 to 14.

The name Satan means adversary, and his ultimate plan is to destroy God and to sit upon God's throne in Heaven. The following scriptures describe who he was originally. An angelic being who wanted only to overthrow God from His heavenly throne. He wanted the honour and worship that only belong to God. He wants everything and everyone to bow down to worship him.

> *Isa 14:12 How art thou fallen from heaven, O Lucifer, son of the morning! how art thou cut down to the ground, which didst weaken the nations!*

> *Isa 14:13 For thou hast said in thine heart, I will ascend into heaven, I will exalt my throne above the stars of God: I will sit also upon the mount of the congregation, in the sides of the north:*

> *Isa 14:14 I will ascend above the heights of the clouds; I will be like the most High.*

Here, Satan has revealed his plans and ambitions. He has spent all his time in trying to bring his plans to completion. He has been actively pursuing this plan from the "Garden of Eden", and every day since.

So it is imperative that we understand what his tactics are, to see what he has tried to do in the past, so we can know what he may try to do in the future, and what tools he has at his disposal.

He works quietly behind the scenes to destroy us in ways that are very subtle and ways that may even seem "Godly". Doing deeds that may appear to be in "God's name" but ever so slightly leading us from the truth and into his trap. We realize that just a little lie mixed in with the truth will cause it all being a lie. This is one tactic of Satan. If he can lead us away from God in just minor issues, then he will try to do the same with larger issues.

We should think about what is revealed to us in. 2Co 11.These verses are best described in the NIV Bible.

2Co 11:10 As the truth of Christ is in me, no man shall stop me of this boasting in the regions of Achaia.

2Co 11:11 Wherefore? because I love you not? God knoweth.

2Co 11:12 But what I do, that I will do, that I may cut off occasion from them which desire occasion; that wherein they glory, they may be found even as we.

2Co 11:13 For such are false apostles, deceitful workers, transforming themselves into the apostles of Christ.

2Co 11:14 And no marvel; for Satan himself is transformed into an angel of light.

Satan is brilliant and uses many tactics in his futile attempts to destroy God, His plans, or His people, Firstly he keeps himself as invisible as possible, and then as we can see in verse 14 above that he pretends to be an angel of light, and the only reason he would do this is to draw us away from God. He has many demons with him and even these demons masquerade as apostles of Christ. We see this in the next verse, verse 15.

2Co 11:15 Therefore it is no great thing if his ministers also be transformed as the ministers of righteousness; whose end shall be according to their works.

Unfortunately, we know these demons will have success at leading people away from the truth of God. This will be even more evident as we come closer to the end of this present age. This will be a time when Satan and his demon friends will be most active and will have outstanding success in accomplishing their plans. We can read of this in 1 Timothy 4:1.

1Ti 4:1 Now the Spirit speaketh expressly, that in the latter times some shall depart from the faith, giving heed to seducing spirits, and doctrines of devils;

So Satan draws people away from God by looking like the real deal, an apostle of Christ, while all the time he leads unwary people away from God. They will influence the many false apostles and ministers who will appear as the time of Christ's return draws near. As the time of Christ's return approaches, they will say to the unwary what they desire to hear, as stated in 2 Timothy 4:3.

2Ti 4:3 For the time will come when they will not endure sound doctrine; but after their own lusts shall they heap to themselves teachers, having itching ears;

These people are not interested in the truth, but only in what they want to hear. They have their own beliefs and will not study God's word to see if what they believe is the truth or not. They would much prefer to listen to half-truths and lies as long as they sound good. Or as the saying goes. "Don't let the truth stand in the way of a wonderful story". Satan is so clever and scheming that it's difficult to tell the truth from his lies.

The only way a Christian will tell what is a lie and what is the truth is, is by being a student of the Bible. Daily study and prayer are the best means of protecting ourselves from Satan and his influence.

We can clearly see the influence of Satan on the world in today's society. Just look at the gay and lesbian movement around the world. Some of these people still attend church services where they are accepted and believe that they are going to heaven when they die. Their "itching ears" want to hear these lies, especially if they come from some ministers of religion. It does not matter what the "Word of God" says, just tell me what I want to hear.

We can clearly see his influence in the teachings of the modern church. The leaders of these institutions tell us all religions lead to heaven. It does not matter what you believe, just as long as you are a good person. This is contrary to the words of God.

In today's age, it's difficult to believe that evil spirits exist, and are everywhere and influence people. But 1 John 4:1-4 warns us to be on our guard against these evil spirits..

> *1Jn 4:1 Beloved, believe not every spirit, but try the spirits whether they are of God: because many false prophets are gone out into the world.*

> *1Jn 4:2 Hereby know ye the Spirit of God: Every spirit that confesseth that Jesus Christ is come in the flesh is of God:*

> *1Jn 4:3 And every spirit that confesseth not that Jesus Christ is come in the flesh is not of God: and this is that spirit of antichrist, whereof ye have heard that it should come; and even now already is it in the world.*

> *1Jn 4:4 Ye are of God, little children, and have overcome them: because greater is he that is in you, than he that is in the world.*

As Christians, we must know the spirit of the Antichrist that has been in the world for hundreds of years, and is causing all our troubles today. Therefore, as children of God, we are to always be on our guard against Satan, the father of lies.

Chapter 3 - Satan's Plan

Satan, Lucifer, or the Devil, whatever name we may give him, has been trying to frustrate the plan of God from the very beginning starting in the Garden of Eden. Satan must have watched in awe and wonder as God created everything in 6 days. But Satan was puffed up with pride. He was created as a guardian cherub, but because of his beauty he became proud and rebelled against God as we read in the first chapter of this book.

In that passage of scripture, we see Satan was created perfect, very wise and perfect in beauty. He became very proud of who he was and of his beauty. Being proud and lofty is a sin against God. So God removed him from his position of authority and cast him to the earth.

During the 6 days God took to create the earth, Satan must have watched and listened to what God told Adam. He would have heard God tell Adam he would surely die if he ate from the tree of the knowledge of good and evil in the middle of the garden as we see in Gen 2:15-17.

Gen 2:15 The LORD God took the man and put him in the Garden of Eden to work it and take care of it.

Gen 2:16 And the LORD God commanded the man, "You are free to eat from any tree in the garden;

Gen 2:17 but you must not eat from the tree of the knowledge of good and evil, for when you eat from it you will certainly die."

Satan was jealous of God and wanted no more then to remove God from his throne. He saw an opportunity here to bring God's plans to nothing. He told Eve she would not die if she ate of the fruit but would instead know good and evil and would be like God himself. Eve believed this lie and ate of the fruit and also gave some to Adam. This is recorded in Gen 3:1-5.

Gen 3:1 Now the serpent was more crafty than any of the wild animals the LORD God had made. He said to the woman, "Did God really say, 'You must not eat from any tree in the garden'?"

Gen 3:2 The woman said to the serpent, "We may eat fruit from the trees in the garden,

Gen 3:3 but God did say, 'You must not eat fruit from the tree that is in the middle of the garden, and you must not touch it, or you will die.'"

Gen 3:4 "You will not certainly die," the serpent said to the woman.

Gen 3:5 "For God knows that when you eat from it your eyes will be opened, and you will be like God, knowing good and evil."

Satan must have thought Adam and Eve would die immediately, he had not planned on them living for many more years and having children. This was no doubt a major disappointment for him. Adam live to be 930 years old. He and Eve had sons and daughters. So this was Satan's first attempt to disrupt God's plans, but he obviously failed, but he never gave up trying and even to this day he is still trying to overpower God.This has always been Satan's plan and he is still trying to accomplish this today. In the following chapters I will discuss how he has tried and failed in the past, and how he will try in the future and no doubt fail again.

Chapter 4 - The Temptation of Jesus Christ

Satan was determined to stop God's plan any way he could. He was determined to prevent Jesus from fulfilling what He had come down to the earth to do. Herod learned from the Magi, or the wise men, when Jesus was born, So he ordered all children in Bethlehem who were under the age of 2 years to be killed. In doing this he hope Jesus would be among those killed. But Joseph had been warned to take Mary and Jesus and flee to Egypt as we see in Mat 2:13-18.

Mat 2:13 When they had gone, an angel of the Lord appeared to Joseph in a dream. "Get up," he said, "take the child and his mother and escape to Egypt. Stay there until I tell you, for Herod is going to search for the child to kill him."

Mat 2:14 So he got up, took the child and his mother during the night and left for Egypt,

Mat 2:15 where he stayed until the death of Herod. And so was fulfilled what the Lord had said through the prophet: "Out of Egypt I called my son."

Mat 2:16 When Herod realized that he had been outwitted by the Magi, he was furious, and he gave orders to kill all the boys in Bethlehem and its vicinity who were two years old and under, in accordance with the time he had learned from the Magi.

Mat 2:17 Then what was said through the prophet Jeremiah was fulfilled:

Mat 2:18 "A voice is heard in Ramah, weeping and great mourning, Rachel weeping for her children and refusing to be comforted, because they are no more."

We know that Herod (no doubt influenced by Satan) tried to have the baby Jesus killed, but Joseph had moved his family to Egypt after being told to do this in a dream from God. Then all male children up to the age of 2 years old in Bethlehem, were killed on orders from Herod to try to destroy the Messiah.

In the previous chapters, we saw some of the arrogance of Satan as he plans to remove God from his throne and occupy it himself. This arrogance is even more evident when he attempted to get Jesus to worship him. As we know he failed miserably again, but he must have thought he had a chance, otherwise he would not have tried to corrupt Jesus.

After Jesus was baptized by John The Baptist, he spent 40 days out in the wilderness and was tempted many times by Satan. Jesus rebuked him every time with a passage from scripture, from what we call the old testament. The new testament had not yet been written.

Satan knew exactly who Jesus was, and also knew if he could get Jesus to worship him instead of The Father, then he would have had a major victory over God. He failed in all of his endeavours. So great was his pride. He actually thought he could change the course of God's plans. Read how he tempted Jesus and how Jesus rebuked him every time with scripture from the old testament.

Mat 4:1 Then Jesus was led by the Spirit into the wilderness to be tempted by the devil.

Mat 4:2 After fasting forty days and forty nights, he was hungry.

Mat 4:3 The tempter came to him and said, "If you are the Son of God, tell these stones to become bread."

Mat 4:4 Jesus answered, "It is written: 'Man shall not live on bread alone, but on every word that comes from the mouth of God.'"

Mat 4:5 Then the devil took him to the holy city and had him stand on the highest point of the temple.

Mat 4:6 "If you are the Son of God," he said, "throw yourself down. For it is written: "'He will command his angels concerning you, and they will

*lift you up in their hands, so that you will not strike your foot against a
stone.'"*

*Mat 4:7 Jesus answered him, "It is also written: 'Do not put the Lord
your God to the test.'"*

*Mat 4:8 Again, the devil took him to a very high mountain and showed
him all the kingdoms of the world and their splendor.*

*Mat 4:9 "All this I will give you," he said, "if you will bow down and
worship me."*

*Mat 4:10 Jesus said to him, "Away from me, Satan! For it is written:
'Worship the Lord your God, and serve him only.'"*

Mat 4:11 Then the devil left him, and angels came and attended him.

Satan was unable to persuade Jesus to bow down to him and have Him comply
with his wishes. So again he failed to upset God's plans. But Satan was not about
to give up even after this. He failed to turn Jesus away from God, so he had
another plan in mind, and that was to have the promised seed, the Messiah,
murdered on the cross.

We learn from Luk 22:3-4 that Satan influenced Judas to betray Jesus to the chief
priests. This was how he was going to destroy the Messiah. Have him crucified.

*Luk 22:3 Then entered Satan into Judas surnamed Iscariot, being of the
number of the twelve.*

*Luk 22:4 And he went his way, and communed with the chief priests and
captains, how he might betray him unto them.*

So Satan thought if he could have Jesus crucified, he would accomplish his plan.

So as we see in verse 3 above, Satan influenced Judas to betray Jesus and have him
arrested, and we know the rest of the story, how Jesus was eventually crucified on

the cross. He must have been very pleased with himself, probably gloating with his fallen angels about how he had finally destroyed God's plan.

I would love to have seen his face three days later when Jesus rose from the tomb, appeared to many people over the next 40 days, and then ascended back into heaven. God had actually used Satan to bring about his plan, so Satan must have been rather upset with this development.

The mission that Jesus set out to do was indeed accomplished. Right before He died His last words are recorded in Joh 19:30.

> *Joh 19:30 When Jesus therefore had received the vinegar, he said, "It is finished." He bowed his head, and gave up his spirit.*

So the plan that God had for humanity was accomplished by Christ's death on the cross. Satan tried to interfere with God's eternal plan. But God actually used Satan to bring about what he had planned all along.

Chapter 5 - The Line Of The Messiah

Satan knows God has a plan to judge him, and that plan involves the Messiah. We see this very early in the Bible in Gen 3:14-15.

Gen 3:14 And the LORD God said unto the serpent, Because thou hast done this, thou art cursed above all cattle, and above every beast of the field; upon thy belly shalt thou go, and dust shalt thou eat all the days of thy life:

Gen 3:15 And I will put enmity between thee and the woman, and between thy seed and her seed; it shall bruise thy head, and thou shalt bruise his heel.

Later, God promised David that there would always be someone from his family line who would sit upon his throne, as we see in 2Sa 7:15-16.

2Sa 7:15 But my mercy shall not depart away from him, as I took it from Saul, whom I put away before thee.

2Sa 7:16 And thine house and thy kingdom shall be established for ever before thee: thy throne shall be established for ever.

Satan knew this and so he made it one of his plans to break this family line, to break the promise God had made to King David. If he could do this, then he would have a major win over God. So Satan was constantly looking for ways to break this family line from King David to the The Messiah.

He almost succeeded in about 840bc. Athaliah, the mother of the evil king Ahaziah attempted to have all of the princes of the royal family slain. She would have succeeded except for the actions of Jehosheba who hid the youngest of the princes. Read this in 2Ch 22:10-12.

2Ch 22:10 When Athaliah the mother of Ahaziah saw that her son was dead, she proceeded to destroy the whole royal family of the house of Judah.

2Ch 22:11 But Jehosheba, the daughter of King Jehoram, took Joash son of Ahaziah and stole him away from among the royal princes who were about to be murdered and put him and his nurse in a bedroom. Because Jehosheba, the daughter of King Jehoram and wife of the priest Jehoiada, was Ahaziah's sister, she hid the child from Athaliah so she could not kill him.

2Ch 22:12 He remained hidden with them at the temple of God for six years while Athaliah ruled the land.

Joash eventually sat upon the throne therefore continuing the royal line from David to Jesus. God did not forget his promise to David, just as he never forgets his promises to us.

Chapter 6 - The Human Race

We all know the story of the "Garden of Eden" and how God created humans in His own image and everything was perfect until Satan came on the scene and was successful in tempting Adam and Eve to sin.

Satan must have thought that if he could get the humans to eat of the tree of Knowledge of good and evil, then God would have no choice but to kill them. Satan believed this because He had heard God speaking to Adam and Eve and declaring they would die if they ate from the tree in the middle of the garden.

> *Gen 2:17 But of the tree of the knowledge of good and evil, thou shalt not eat of it: for in the day that thou eatest thereof thou shalt surely die.*

This was Satan's first mistake, he must have assumed that their deaths would be immediate and this would have been the end of humanity. But God allowed Adam and Eve to have children and multiply upon the earth, and only then did they die. So humans continued, and Satan failed in his first attempt to scuttle God's plans.

When Cain killed Able, he probably thought he had a victory at last, but Adam and Eve had another son, Seth, who is a part of the royal family line right up to Jesus. This is recorded in the third chapter of Luke verses 23 to 38, where Christ's genealogy is traced right back to Adam and Eve, and in verse 38, at the end of the genealogy list we see Seth is named in the list.

> *Luk 3:38 Which was the son of Enos, which was the son of Seth, which was the son of Adam, which was the son of God.*

Seth is in the line of ancestors of Jesus. Cain and Able were not. So Satan failed in his plan to end the royal line to Jesus. This royal line from Adam to Jesus was not broken, and Satan failed again in his plans.

By the time of Noah, humanity had sunk to an all-time low, no doubt influenced by Satan, and God was tempted to destroy all life on earth. This part of the story we can read about in Gen 6:5-13.

Gen 6:5 Yahweh saw that the wickedness of man was great in the earth, and that every imagination of the thoughts of man's heart was continually only evil.

Gen 6:6 Yahweh was sorry that he had made man on the earth, and it grieved him in his heart.

Gen 6:7 Yahweh said, "I will destroy man whom I have created from the surface of the ground—man, along with animals, creeping things, and birds of the sky—for I am sorry that I have made them."

Up to this point, Satan must have been feeling happy with himself and looking forward to seeing how God would accomplish the destruction of all human life from the earth. But he was not anticipating what was to follow starting in verse 8.

Gen 6:8 But Noah found favor in Yahweh's eyes.

Gen 6:9 This is the history of the generations of Noah: Noah was a righteous man, blameless among the people of his time. Noah walked with God.

Gen 6:10 Noah became the father of three sons: Shem, Ham, and Japheth.

Gen 6:11 The earth was corrupt before God, and the earth was filled with violence.

Gen 6:12 God saw the earth, and saw that it was corrupt, for all flesh had corrupted their way on the earth.

Gen 6:13 God said to Noah, "I will bring an end to all flesh, for the earth is filled with violence through them. Behold, I will destroy them and the earth.

So God instructed Noah how to build the ark to save himself and the animals God wanted to save to repopulate the earth after the flood. Thankfully, Noah found favour with God, and built the ark. otherwise we would not be here today, but God decided to save Noah and his family, but to destroy the rest of earth's population. So God sent a Flood to destroy the entire world, except for Noah and his family. So humanity was spared, and Satan's dream of humanity being totally destroyed failed again.

Now Satan has to bide his time and wait for another chance to upset God's plans.

Chapter 7 - Job's Temptation

Many people do not realize that Satan travels between Heaven and the Earth. He has had this ability from the time he was created. The day is coming, and maybe not that far away, when he will be kicked out of Heaven totally and never be able to return.

The book of Job makes it very clear that Satan can actually do this. This book also reveals to us that he can do no more than what God allows him to do. We know from the story of Job that Satan had to get permission from God to bring troubles to Job. Satan accused Job of only being loyal to God because God had given him so many blessings. God knew better than this, so He allowed Satan to bring many disasters on Job in an attempt to make him curse God. We also learn from this book that he could do only what God allowed. This proves to us that God has the ultimate power, and Satan is restricted in everything he does.

We can read the story of Job and see how Satan can do nothing without God's permission. Job 1:6-12 explains this very well.

Job 1:6 Now there was a day when the sons of God came to present themselves before the LORD, and Satan came also among them.

Job 1:7 And the LORD said unto Satan, Whence comest thou? Then Satan answered the LORD, and said, From going to and fro in the earth, and from walking up and down in it.

Job 1:8 And the LORD said unto Satan, Hast thou considered my servant Job, that there is none like him in the earth, a perfect and an upright man, one that feareth God, and escheweth evil?

Job 1:9 Then Satan answered the LORD, and said, Doth Job fear God for nought?

Job 1:10 Hast not thou made an hedge about him, and about his house, and about all that he hath on every side? thou hast blessed the work of his hands, and his substance is increased in the land.

Job 1:11 But put forth thine hand now, and touch all that he hath, and he will curse thee to thy face.

Job 1:12 And the LORD said unto Satan, Behold, all that he hath is in thy power; only upon himself put not forth thine hand. So Satan went forth from the presence of the LORD.

We know that Satan then went out and took everything that Job had including all of his livestock and even had Job's children killed, so Job was left with nothing, everything he owned was taken away from him, this must have been a very low point in Job's life, and he was wondering why these calamities had come upon him. But no harm came to Job himself.

Even with everything that Job held dear was taken away from him, he never cursed God or spoke a careless word against Him.

Then Satan came before God again and claimed that Job would curse God, if he was personally afflicted. So God gave Satan permission to bring troubles onto Job personally, to try to make him curse God. But he was not given the power to kill him, only to cause him as much grief as he could. We see this in Job chapter 2 and verses 6 and 7:

Job 2:6 And the LORD said unto Satan, Behold, he is in thine hand; but save his life.

Job 2:7 So went Satan forth from the presence of the LORD, and smote Job with sore boils from the sole of his foot unto his crown.

So Satan could not do more to Job than what God allowed. His powers to harm Job were restricted, and it is still the same today in everything. Satan is permitted just so much power and influence over the world, but no more. Ultimately, God is in complete control.

After all of the troubles Job went through, God blessed him again and he was once again a very wealthy man and he had 10 more children to replace those Satan had killed. Read the following verse to see just how much God blessed Job.

Job 42:10 After Job had prayed for his friends, the LORD restored his fortunes and gave him twice as much as he had before.

Job 42:11 All his brothers and sisters and everyone who had known him before came and ate with him in his house. They comforted and consoled him over all the trouble the LORD had brought on him, and each one gave him a piece of silver and a gold ring.

Job 42:12 The LORD blessed the latter part of Job's life more than the former part. He had fourteen thousand sheep, six thousand camels, a thousand yoke of oxen and a thousand donkeys.

Job 42:13 And he also had seven sons and three daughters.

Job 42:14 The first daughter he named Jemimah, the second Keziah and the third Keren-Happuch.

Job 42:15 Nowhere in all the land were there found women as beautiful as Job's daughters, and their father granted them an inheritance along with their brothers.

Job 42:16 After this, Job lived a hundred and forty years; he saw his children and their children to the fourth generation.

Job 42:17 And so Job died, an old man and full of years.

We can all learn from Job's experience. Yes, Satan is real and has a lot of power, but he can only do what God allows him to do.

Chapter 8 - The Jewish Nation

The next target of Satan was to destroy the nation of Israel. In Gen 12;1-3 God promised Abraham that he would be the father of many people and that the earth would be blessed because of him.

Gen 12:1 Now Yahweh said to Abram, "Leave your country, and your relatives, and your father's house, and go to the land that I will show you.

Gen 12:2 I will make of you a great nation. I will bless you and make your name great. You will be a blessing.

Gen 12:3 I will bless those who bless you, and I will curse him who treats you with contempt. All the families of the earth will be blessed through you."

God promised that the descendants of Abraham would exist forever. If the nation that came from Abraham's descendants, Israel, were ever annihilated as a nation, then the Word of God would be untrue. It is for this reason that Satan has paid special attention to Abraham's descendants even to this very day.

In the Book of Esther, we have an example of the attempted destruction of the entire Jewish nation. This book was written between the years 331bc and 560bc by an unknown author. King Xerxes was looking for a new wife and chose Esther, a Jewess, to be his new queen. Mordecai was her uncle and guardian and had instructed Esther not to tell anyone she was a Jew.

At this time Mordecai heard of a plot to assassinate the king, he warned Esther of the plot who advised the king. The plot was uncovered and the men responsible were hanged. After this, king Xerxes honoured a man called Haman to a higher rank than any other nobleman. He passed a degree that everyone was to bow down to him when ever he passed by. But Mordecai, being a Jew who only bowed down to God, refused to bow down to Haman.

This act of defiance infuriated Haman and he had the king sign a decree and send it to all parts of his kingdom to have all Jewish people destroyed! We read this is Est 3:12 to 14.

> *Est 3:12 Then the king's scribes were called in on the first month, on the thirteenth day of the month; and all that Haman commanded was written to the king's local governors, and to the governors who were over every province, and to the princes of every people, to every province according to its writing, and to every people in their language. It was written in the name of King Ahasuerus, and it was sealed with the king's ring.*

> *Est 3:13 Letters were sent by couriers into all the king's provinces, to destroy, to kill, and to cause to perish, all Jews, both young and old, little children and women, in one day, even on the thirteenth day of the twelfth month, which is the month Adar, and to plunder their possessions.*

> *Est 3:14 A copy of the letter, that the decree should be given out in every province, was published to all the peoples, that they should be ready against that day.*

Again, Satan must have thought that he had had a victory over God by having the entire Jewish population killed.

Haman's plan came unstuck when Queen Esther (who was Jewish) threw a banquet for the King and Haman, and then revealed to the King what Haman had planned for the Jewish people, and this would have included Esther as well. We can pick up the story from Est 7:1-6.

> *Est 7:1 So the king and Haman came to banquet with Esther the queen.*

> *Est 7:2 The king said again to Esther on the second day at the banquet of wine, "What is your petition, queen Esther? It shall be granted you. What is your request? Even to the half of the kingdom it shall be performed."*

Est 7:3 Then Esther the queen answered, "If I have found favor in your sight, O king, and if it pleases the king, let my life be given me at my petition, and my people at my request.

Est 7:4 For we are sold, I and my people, to be destroyed, to be slain, and to perish. But if we had been sold for male and female slaves, I would have held my peace, although the adversary could not have compensated for the king's loss."

Est 7:5 Then King Ahasuerus said to Esther the queen, "Who is he, and where is he who dared presume in his heart to do so?"

Est 7:6 Esther said, "An adversary and an enemy, even this wicked Haman!" Then Haman was afraid before the king and the queen.

Haman did not know Esther was a Jew, otherwise he may have acted differently. But Mordecai had advise Esther not to tell anyone that she was a Jew. Haman was out to get revenge on Mordecai for not bowing down to him as he rode past on his horse. His plan was to rid the land of all Jews including Mordecai. His greatest mistake was in not realising who Esther was. So when Esther held the banquet for the King and for Haman, she pleaded for her own life and for the lives of the Jews as verses 3 and 4 tell us.

When Esther made it known to the king that she herself was a Jew. Haman must have started to fear for his own safety and no doubt he was now regretting the plot he had planned to have all Jews killed just for revenge on Mordecai.

Subsequently, Haman was hanged on the gallows he had purposefully built for Mordecai, and the decree to have the entire Jewish nation annihilated was reversed, therefore saving them all from destruction. So the Jewish nation is still with us today.

Even today we still see Satan trying his best to eliminate the Jewish Nation. Can you imagine what would have become of the Jews if Hitler had won the second world war. He had millions of Jews murdered in the gas chambers, but could not accomplish his ultimate aim of a total annihilation of the Jewish People.

Satan failed again.

Chapter 9 - Satan Tempts King David

King David has been described as a man after God's own heart, yet he was tempted by Satan to do what was wrong in the eyes of God. He sent Joab, one of his generals, out into Israel for a census. Joab knew it was wrong to do this, so David must have known also, but as we read in 1Ch 21:1-3, Satan incited or persuaded David to carry out the census.

1Ch 21:1 Satan rose up against Israel and incited David to take a census of Israel.

1Ch 21:2 So David said to Joab and the commanders of the troops, "Go and count the Israelites from Beersheba to Dan. Then report back to me so that I may know how many there are."

1Ch 21:3 But Joab replied, "May the LORD multiply his troops a hundred times over. My lord the king, are they not all my lord's subjects? Why does my lord want to do this? Why should he bring guilt on Israel?"

It is interesting to note, Joab was totally against this census being carried out and spoke against his King. He was aware it was a sin against God to do this, but King David insisted. David must have known it was wrong, the same as Joab did. But Satan convinced him to go ahead with the census anyway.

The penalty for this sin against God was severe as we can see in verses 13-14 below.

1Ch 21:13 David said to Gad, "I am in deep distress. Let me fall into the hands of the LORD, for his mercy is very great; but do not let me fall into human hands."

1Ch 21:14 So the LORD sent a plague on Israel, and seventy thousand men of Israel fell dead.

When David ordered the census, he was acting out of pride. And pride is one of the greatest sins anyone can commit before God. It was pride that caused the downfall of Satan, as we can see in Isaiah 14:13-14.

Isa 14:13 You said in your heart, "I will ascend into heaven! I will exalt my throne above the stars of God! I will sit on the mountain of assembly, in the far north!"

Isa 14:14 I will ascend above the heights of the clouds! I will make myself like the Most High!"

All of God's elect, no matter how good they may be, can never be safe from Satan's influence. Indeed, the more a person wants to live according to God's ways. The more he can expect Satan to be lurking in the shadows, waiting for his chance to cause corruption. Maybe if you are not being targeted by Satan, you are not doing enough to warrant his attention.

Chapter 10 - Satan Blocks Paul

When we think of the Apostle Paul, we think of a person who has great faith, who performed miracles and was not afraid of the Pharisees, but was fearless in his spreading of the gospel. He is the author of about a third of the new testament. Yet he was still blocked by the power of Satan from going to visit the Thessalonians. We read in 1Th 2:17-20.

> *1Th 2:17 But, brothers and sisters, when we were orphaned by being separated from you for a short time (in person, not in thought), out of our intense longing we made every effort to see you.*
>
> *1Th 2:18 For we wanted to come to you—certainly I, Paul, did, again and again—but Satan blocked our way.*
>
> *1Th 2:19 For what is our hope, our joy, or the crown in which we will glory in the presence of our Lord Jesus when he comes? Is it not you?*
>
> *1Th 2:20 Indeed, you are our glory and joy.*

It is an amazing fact that even for Paul, with his ministry and authority that he could be blocked by Satan and not just once, but as we read in verse 18, Paul wanted to go to the Thessalonians many times, but each time he was blocked by Satan. We do not know how Satan did this, but Paul attributes the fact that he could not visit the Thessalonians to something that Satan did to impede his visits.

Even though Paul could not visit them, he got his message to these people. Simply by writing them a letter. And this is where we can be very thankful that Satan did block Paul. Without him blocking Paul, we may have never had this letter written and preserved for us today. So Satan did us a good turn by his actions, and today we have this letter to the Thessalonians with its invaluable information in our Bibles.

Satan must really regret having blocked Paul and seeing Paul's letter spread further around the world. It is amazing how when Satan tries to stop something from happening, God will use Satan's efforts to bring about an even greater good.

But Paul obviously kept on trying to visit the Thessalonians, and, in the end, he was successful. By his persistence, he could remove Satan's blockade, and he eventually got to visit with the Thessalonians.

It seems Satan was desperately trying to keep Paul and his companions away from the new church at Thessalonica, maybe he thought since they were new and relatively weak, he may be able to destroy the church.

Satan has always had a fierce hatred of the gospel, or the good news from being preached. He also hates to see good Christian fellowship and this would be just another reason why he tried to stop Paul from visiting the Thessalonians. Satan wants to keep Christians apart from each other where they would become much easier prey for him and his demons to corrupt. He knows that together we are stronger than we are as individuals

Chapter 11 - Satan Detains the Angel

Satan delayed Paul from visiting the Thessalonians as we saw in the last chapter. In this chapter we will see how "The prince of the kingdom of Persia" delayed an angel as he was on his way to deliver a message to Daniel. This prince may be Satan himself, or one of his evil spiritual minions who wielded some sort of authority over Persia.

The angel was delayed by this prince for 21 days. It is interesting to note here that as soon as Daniel set his heart to understand what this vision meant, the angel was sent from God as verse 12 reveals to us. But he was detained for 21 days. He finally gets the help he needs from Michael, one of the chief princes so he can continue on his journey to Daniel.

We must always remember that our main fight is not against flesh and blood as we see every day around the world. Our fight is against the spiritual wickedness in high places as we see in Eph 6:12.

> *Eph 6:12 For we wrestle not against flesh and blood, but against principalities, against powers, against the rulers of the darkness of this world, against spiritual wickedness in high places.*

Daniel received a vision that troubled him a great deal and he spent 21 days in mourning as he tried to understand the vision recorded in Dan 10:3.

> *Dan 10:3 I ate no pleasant bread, neither came flesh nor wine in my mouth, neither did I anoint myself at all, till three whole weeks were fulfilled.*

Daniel was trying to understand what this vision meant for 21 days.

In the following section of scripture, we see Satan. "The prince of the kingdom of Persia", trying to interfere yet again with God's work. An angel, sent from God to Daniel the prophet to reveal to him part of the future was held up for twenty-one days, and only with the help of Michael, one of God's mighty angels, was the angel able to continue to Daniel with the message he was given by God.

Dan 10:10 And, behold, an hand touched me, which set me upon my knees and upon the palms of my hands.

Dan 10:11 And he said unto me, O Daniel, a man greatly beloved, understand the words that I speak unto thee, and stand upright: for unto thee am I now sent. And when he had spoken this word unto me, I stood trembling.

Dan 10:12 Then said he unto me, Fear not, Daniel: for from the first day that thou didst set thine heart to understand, and to chasten thyself before thy God, thy words were heard, and I am come for thy words.

Dan 10:13 But the prince of the kingdom of Persia withstood me one and twenty days: but, lo, Michael, one of the chief princes, came to help me; and I remained there with the kings of Persia.

Dan 10:14 Now I am come to make thee understand what shall befall thy people in the latter days: for yet the vision is for many days.

We can see from these chapters that Satan had the power to delay both Paul and this angel. Therefore, we must understand that he also has some power over Christians today to try to divert the work of God. He will try to divide us and do all he can to draw us away from our Lord. It is up to us to keep close to Jesus through regular prayers, bible studies and helping our fellow man wherever we can.

Chapter 12 - Satan Hinders Christians

If Satan could block Paul, then how much more will he be able to block us from doing what we know to be right? It is a fact that if we expect success in our Christian lives, then we should also expect to hear some rumbling from Satan in the background trying to block us.

Our path to the Kingdom is fraught with many trials and temptations. We have never been told our path would be easy, but in fact, the very opposite is true. We are told to expect troubles of all kinds in this world.

When we conclude that whatever is hindering us is from Satan, then what can and should we do? We should do as Paul did. We should continue on our path towards our calling in God as the Holy Spirit enables us, regardless of what Satan tries to do to derail us from our destination. To stop is to give in to Satan. To continue is to please God.

I believe that when the Devil is quiet and not causing us any trouble. Then this is probably a sign that we are not doing much to upset him. But when we are being slandered, and the world seems to hate us, and our names are mud to the rest of the world, then we must be doing something that upsets Satan.

We cannot do anything good and worthwhile to advance the gospel, and not expect opposition from our enemy. So when we feel that hindrance from Satan, we must expect to have a fight on our hands, and then we will not be disappointed. If we go through a full year with no resistance from Satan, then he probably thought that we were not worth the effort and he would find someone else worth attacking.

We must preach the gospel of Jesus Christ with all of our strength, soul and might. We can be certain if we do this we will be hated by the rest of the world. That should not worry us, it is a sure sign Satan is trying to hinder us.

We must be aware of the fact that Satan is always on the lookout for people to draw away from God. It is his ambition to destroy everything that is of God as we see in the following verse.

1Pe 5:8 Be alert and of sober mind. Your enemy the devil prowls around like a roaring lion looking for someone to devour.

If there is one lesson to learn from this book, then this is it. Satan is a past master at using people and circumstances to alter the path God has set out for you. John Calvin said it very well when he said. "Whenever the ungodly cause us trouble, they are fighting under the banner of Satan, and are his instruments for harassing us."

Naturally, these people will not realise they are under Satan's banner, but that does not change the fact that they are.

There will be times in your life when you may feel compelled to speak to someone. To do a certain service for a friend or neighbour. But you do not do it. This may just be Satan's way of obstructing you. This is when you must learn to resist Satan.

Chapter 13 - Satan Attacks The Churches

So the plan of God has been accomplished this far despite all the efforts and strategies that Satan used to stop Him. And today we see the Church is still spreading the gospel of Jesus around the world. So now we see Satan attacking the church and using his fallen angels masquerading as ministers of light and drawing many people away from the truth. But there is still some who follow Christ faithfully, so again Satan has failed, but the church must be on its guard, especially as the end draws near because this is when Satan will be at his most powerful and will do his level best to destroy Christ's church.

In Revelation, chapter 12 and verses 12 to 17 we see how Satan is hurled to the earth and is then intent on destroying the church.

> *Rev 12:12 Therefore rejoice, heavens, and you who dwell in them. Woe to the earth and to the sea, because the devil has gone down to you, having great wrath, knowing that he has but a short time."*

> *Rev 12:13 When the dragon saw that he was thrown down to the earth, he persecuted the woman who gave birth to the male child.*

> *Rev 12:14 Two wings of the great eagle were given to the woman, that she might fly into the wilderness to her place, so that she might be nourished for a time, and times, and half a time, from the face of the serpent.*

> *Rev 12:15 The serpent spewed water out of his mouth after the woman like a river, that he might cause her to be carried away by the stream.*

> *Rev 12:16 The earth helped the woman, and the earth opened its mouth and swallowed up the river which the dragon spewed out of his mouth.*

> *Rev 12:17 The dragon grew angry with the woman, and went away to make war with the rest of her offspring, who keep God's commandments and hold Jesus' testimony.*

So far we see Satan has tried to destroy the human race. After failing this he turned his attention to the Messiah's promised line from Adam through to the birth of Jesus. Then he attempted to destroy God's chosen people, the Jewish nation. Next, he targeted the mission of Jesus on the earth, and then we see he is still actively pursuing the Church that Jesus established. In all of his planning and scheming Satan has failed to stop God's plan, he has lost, and Jesus has defeated him and his demons at every turn.

So Satan's target today is to destroy the church. He will do this by masquerading as an angel of light while deceiving people into believing false teachings, and as the end time draws near his powers will increase, and he will perform many amazing deeds that will convince many people throughout the world that his powers are from God, or that he is indeed God.

Today we see Satan at his work trying his best to destroy God's church. He wants to entice us all away from following Jesus, and he will do everything that he can to accomplish this. We must always remember that we are fighting against an enemy we cannot see and whose presence we cannot feel.

Therefore, we are advised to put on the full Armour of God as described in Ephesians. Putting on the full Armour of God simply means that the pieces of the armor are found in a relationship with Jesus. In Romans 13:14 Paul tells us to "Put on the Lord Jesus Christ", This is the same as putting on His Armour. When we give ourselves to Jesus and "put on" His righteousness, we are clothed in the whole armor of God.

If we do this, then we must be able to say what Paul wrote in 2 Tim 4:7-8

> *2Ti 4:7 I have fought the good fight. I have finished the course. I have kept the faith.*

> *2Ti 4:8 From now on, there is stored up for me the crown of righteousness, which the Lord, the righteous judge, will give to me on that day; and not to me only, but also to all those who have loved his appearing.*

When these times of trouble arrive (and they surely will) then the Christians living will need to have the courage and faith to resist Satan and his demons. They must not shy away from danger but remain loyal to God as instructed in.

> *1Co 15:58 Therefore, my beloved brothers, be steadfast, immovable, always abounding in the Lord's work, because you know that your labor is not in vain in the Lord.*

And again in.

> *1Co 16:13 Watch! Stand firm in the faith! Be courageous! Be strong!*

This will certainly be a time of testing, when Christians will have to choose who to follow. Trust God enough to die for their convictions, or give up the race halfway through and suffer the consequences.

The battle that Satan is waging is a very real one, even though it is a very one sided battle, he will never give up his ambitions to tip God off His throne, he just does not know when he has been beaten.

Satan is very active in the world today and is attacking the church in 2 ways. First he attacks from the inside while at the same time attacking the church from the outside. Satan actively attacks the church from the inside by introducing false teachings. This is made evident to us in 1Ti 4:1-2.

> *1Ti 4:1 Now the Spirit speaketh expressly, that in the latter times some shall depart from the faith, giving heed to seducing spirits, and doctrines of devils;*

> *1Ti 4:2 Speaking lies in hypocrisy; having their conscience seared with a hot iron;*

Notice it is in the "latter days" that some will depart from the truth by following the doctrines of devils and seducing spirits who will speak the lies of hypocrisy. This truth is also revealed to us in 2Co 11:14-15.

2Co 11:14 And no marvel; for Satan himself is transformed into an angel of light.

2Co 11:15 Therefore it is no great thing if his ministers also be transformed as the ministers of righteousness; whose end shall be according to their works.

These ministers of Satan, ministers of false doctrines who speak lies of hypocrisy are active in churches today. We see cults forming and large churches teaching just what their congregations want to hear, not necessarily the truth, but only what their "itching ears" want to hear. One of the greatest lies they spread is that of a pre-tribulation rapture. Many of the large churches spread this false teaching because it is what their people want to hear, and since they are the ones supporting these churches financially, the pastors say what they want to hear.

When Jesus returns in all power and glory, He will not even deal with the defeated Satan Himself. Rather, He will send one of His loyal angels to bind him and throw him into the abyss.

In Rev 20:1 and 2 we see where Satan is finally stopped and put where he can no longer cause any of God's children any pain and suffering.

May the day that this angel carries out this task is with us soon. In the meantime we must know Satan is lurking about looking for people to devour (lead away from God) We know Jesus has overcome the world, death and Satan. So let us continue to trust Jesus in all things and follow His lead.

Chapter 1 4 - Satan Leads The Whole World Astray

We are now living in a time when the "Woke" generation, the world economic forum, and the United Nations wants us all to conform to whatever their agenda might be. They will never accept that people have a right to our own thoughts and beliefs. They generally hate religion and all churches and would close them all down if they were given the opportunity. They tell us we must go along with their ideas on matters of government, marriage, sexuality, and the education of our children.

Christians who believe they should follow the teachings of our Lord from the bible will always have a different perspective on any of these matters. They will know what is right and what is wrong and must stand firm in their commitment to obey God rather than the teachings of man. This is when Christians must understand the concept of "Do Not Conform" that has been made clear in the new testament.

> *Rom 12:2 Do not conform to the pattern of this world, but be transformed by the renewing of your mind. Then you will be able to test and approve what God's will is—his good, pleasing and perfect will.*

To conform to the ways of this world is easy. Just fall in line with everything you hear from those who are constantly demanding we change to fit into their living standards. The following scriptures tell us what the conditions of mankind will be like in the last days. I believe that time is rapidly approaching. The behaviour of many in our modern society fits in well with the descriptions given below.

> *2Ti 3:1 This know also, that in the last days perilous times shall come.*

> *2Ti 3:2 For men shall be lovers of their own selves, covetous, boasters, proud, blasphemers, disobedient to parents, unthankful, unholy,*

> *2Ti 3:3 Without natural affection, trucebreakers, false accusers, incontinent, fierce, despisers of those that are good,*

2Ti 3:4 Traitors, heady, highminded, lovers of pleasures more than lovers of God;

2Ti 3:5 Having a form of godliness, but denying the power thereof: from such turn away.

Revelation 12:9 clearly tells us Satan has deceived the whole world and he is the author of confusion. Take an honest look at the conditions of the world. There is turmoil everywhere. Wars are raging in many parts of the world. Governments are forcing their policies on those they are opposed to be serving. The world economic forum is trying to take control of the finances of every man, woman and child on the earth. The United Nations seeks to rule over all governments.

These conditions are all in accordance with the plans of Satan. What is happening in the world today is a very clear picture that we have given this world over to Satan. I know many of you will disagree with me, but wait a few years and see what the outcome will be for us all.

The people of this world have rejected God from almost every part of their lives. He is not welcome in Governments, schools, or most establishments. Even many of the churches have bowed down to the "Woke generation" of this world, and have watered down the teachings of the bible. What was once right, is now wrong. What was once good is now evil and evil has taken the place of the good.

Yes, Satan is very real, the proof is all around you if you are prepared to look. There is a great deal we do not know about this powerful spiritual being. But we know from the word of God that he is ultimately behind all evil on this earth.

There are three truths that you can believe about Satan. First he is real and powerful. He is not some impersonal spirit being or force. He has a personality and he schemes, plans, and plots against us every day.

The second thing we can believe about him is he is opposed to all of God's plans for his chosen people. He will do all in his power to destroy us given the chance.

The last point to make here is he is also a defeated enemy. When Jesus died on the cross he broke all holds Satan has over us. We must keep this in mind and remain loyal to our Saviour Jesus Christ.

Chapter 15 - Satan is Targeting Man's Free will

One of the greatest blessings God has given to mankind is also the one that Satan will use to attack us, and to draw us away from our God. From the very beginning, God gave Adam and Eve free will to make their own choices. So when the serpent told Eve she could eat of the tree of knowledge of good and evil, and not die, she believed him and made her own choice to eat of the forbidden fruit. Yes, Satan tempted her, but in the end she ate of the fruit, and so did Adam. It was their own free will to do this.

God could have prevented this from happening, but then their free wills would have been taken away from them. They would have been forced to comply with God's wishes. But God did not intervene because He wants all people to come to Him, to love, worship and to obey Him of their own choosing. He will force none of us to do what is right. We make that decision for ourselves, exactly the same way Adam and Eve had to make their own decisions.

Obviously, having this same free will is going to leave us open to make mistakes the same way Adam and Eve did. But God will have it no other way. If He set up and forced us to live within certain boundaries that we must comply with, then He would have just created another herd of cows, sheep, goats or any other animal He created. Each living by certain laws God created for their particular type of animal. Each after its own kind was recorded for us in.

Gen 1:25 And God made the beast of the earth after his kind, and cattle after their kind, and every thing that creepeth upon the earth after his kind: and God saw that it was good.

Let us take one example from the animal world. Sheep can only do what all sheep do. They cannot do any of the amazing things God created humans to do. They have a very set way to live and have no free will to change their circumstances. And as Gen 1:25 tells us, each will behave according to its kind. It is only humans who have is amazing free will that allows us to pursue different things in our lives.

So how does Satan use our free will against us?

The first thing to keep in mind is that Satan is not only very real, but he also has great power. Unfortunately, many people do not think he is real, or that he may have some sort of sway over their lives. They see him as powerless and unable to influence anyone. This is exactly what he wants us to believe. If we do not see him as a threat, he can continue to draw us away from God without our even being aware of his presence. But he is real and wants nothing more than to corrupt humans. Read about his presence and his plan in the following words from God's Bible.

> *Job 1:7 And the LORD said unto Satan, Whence comest thou? Then Satan answered the LORD, and said, From going to and fro in the earth, and from walking up and down in it.*

Also in.

> *1Pe 5:8 Be sober, be vigilant; because your adversary the devil, as a roaring lion, walketh about, seeking whom he may devour:*

In these two verses, we plainly see two very important details. First, Satan roams over the entire earth, and second, he is looking for people to devour. This means people to corrupt and draw away from God. So now let us look at how he does this.

Satan certainly understands the enormous power contained within our "free will". He used his own free will when he and his demons first rebelled against God. His pride made him make the wrong decisions and now he is determined to take over God's throne.

In this current time, we face an enormous amount of distractions designed to draw us away from God. I will name but a few here and leave you all to add whatever you like.

Lets us start with football in all of its different formats, soccer, grid iron and Aussie rules. How many people would much rather watch one of these sports, whether in person or on the television, than to study the Bible? The number would be in the multiple millions, and I dare to suggest it will actually be in the billions. Now consider how many other sports will accomplish Satan's task of drawing people away from God. Every sport has its own band of regular followers who "religiously" follow their teams.

Please note here that I am not advocating that all sport is wrong. It is only wrong if it consumes all of your spare time and leaves no time for God. Sport is a healthy pastime, but it should never interfere with your time with God. Nor am I saying you should study the word of God every spare hour you have. You need to strike a healthy balance between the two. But your time with God should always be more important to you than anything else.

Next, we need to see how many of us will be distracted through our work. This one is a bit more difficult, as some are forced to work long hours just to survive. Finding time for God is not so easy when your family depends on your income so much. But there are many others who work long hours simply for the money, and for what it can buy for their own pleasures. There are many people who would rather be at work than try to get to know their God.

In this modern age, we have one of the greatest distractions of all. The one we call "social media". This one is anything but social and is one area where there is an inordinate amount of evil. The poisonous comments left on other peoples face book pages are shocking, and there are many people who spend most of their days trolling these pages to find someone to disagree with.

The Internet is a fantastic place to find just about any information you want to broaden your mind. But again, people waste their time as they search for the wrong things.

Even church will draw people away from God. This may sound like a contradiction, but there are churches who teach heresy and the teaching of men rather than the word of God. Satan is more than happy to use this as a distraction from the truth. Consider the following passage of scripture.

> *2Co 11:13 For such are false apostles, deceitful workers, transforming themselves into the apostles of Christ.*

> *2Co 11:14 And no marvel; for Satan himself is transformed into an angel of light.*

2Co 11:15 Therefore it is no great thing if his ministers also be transformed as the ministers of righteousness; whose end shall be according to their works.

Satan will do whatever it takes to entice you away from God and the amazing reward you will get if you stay loyal to Him. He is even happy to look like he is a religious leader as long as he can inject heresy and false teachings along the way. We are instructed to resist the devil, and the only way we can do this is by seeking knowledge and understanding from the scriptures. There is no other way. This is shown to us in Eph 6:10-17.

Eph 6:10 Finally, be strong in the Lord and in his mighty power.

Eph 6:11 Put on the full armor of God, so that you can take your stand against the devil's schemes.

Eph 6:12 For our struggle is not against flesh and blood, but against the rulers, against the authorities, against the powers of this dark world and against the spiritual forces of evil in the heavenly realms.

Eph 6:13 Therefore put on the full armor of God, so that when the day of evil comes, you may be able to stand your ground, and after you have done everything, to stand.

Eph 6:14 Stand firm then, with the belt of truth buckled around your waist, with the breastplate of righteousness in place,

Eph 6:15 and with your feet fitted with the readiness that comes from the gospel of peace.

Eph 6:16 In addition to all this, take up the shield of faith, with which you can extinguish all the flaming arrows of the evil one.

Eph 6:17 Take the helmet of salvation and the sword of the Spirit, which is the word of God.

See how these verses end with. "Which is the word of God." So putting on all of this full armour of God is actually done by reading and learning from the word of God, or His holy Bible.

We all have our own free will for how we will spend our time. It is our choice to watch sport, work harder than we should just to earn more money. We can spend hours every day on computers to find someone we can disagree with and leave evil comments on their pages. Or we can use any spare time to get to know God from His written word, the Bible.

This is a decision we must all make for ourselves. I sincerely hope you choose to spend time in God's words. There is a great deal to learn, so do not be discouraged, but learn a little every day and grow in the grace and knowledge of Jesus Christ.

Chapter 16 - Resist The Devil

Satan has certain powers but they are infinitely less powerful than that of our Almighty God. We are informed in Jas 4:7 that the way to defeat Satan is to resist him by submitting ourselves to God. This verse also informs us what Satan will do if we submit ourselves to God. He will flee from us.

Jas 4:7 Be subject therefore to God. Resist the devil, and he will flee from you.

This is reinforced in Eph 4:27

Eph 4:27 Neither give place to the devil.

Now we must ask the question. "How do we overcome Satan and his lies? We have already read we must put on the full armour of God to protect ourselves. But we also have more advice and that is from

Rev 12:11 And they overcame him by the blood of the Lamb, and by the word of their testimony; and they loved not their lives unto the death.

To triumph over him by the blood of the Lamb simply means to be a follower of Jesus, to live by His laws and the resist Satan at all costs. This means to remain faithful even in the face of death. It is better to die in faith, than to give in to Satan and end up with him and his demons in the eternal fire.

Unfortunately, most of the world's population does not see Satan as any sort of threat to their way of life or their future. They do not recognise he is the enemy of God, and our enemy as well. He is very active in this world and that is why he is called the "prince of the earth" among other names. We are warned to be on guard against Satan and his henchmen, who are always on the lookout for a way to disrupt what God has in mind for his people.

Absolutely no one is exempt from his attempts to disrupt our plans or to influence our thoughts and draw us away from God.

In the following section of scripture, we again see Satan. "The prince of the kingdom of Persia", trying to interfere with God's work. An angel sent from God to Daniel to reveal to him part of the future.

The angel was held up for twenty-one days, and only with the help of Michael, one of God's mighty angels, was the angel able to continue to Daniel with the message he was given by God.

> *1Th 2:10 Behold, a hand touched me, which set me on my knees and on the palms of my hands.*

> *1Th 2:11 He said to me, Daniel, you greatly beloved man, understand the words that I speak to you, and stand upright; for I have been sent to you, now. When he had spoken this word to me, I stood trembling.*

> *1Th 2:12 Then he said to me, "Don't be afraid, Daniel; for from the first day that you set your heart to understand, and to humble yourself before your God, your words were heard. I have come for your words' sake.*

> *1Th 2:13 But the prince of the kingdom of Persia withstood me twenty-one days; but, behold, Michael, one of the chief princes, came to help me because I remained there with the kings of Persia.*

> *1Th 2:14 Now I have come to make you understand what will happen to your people in the latter days; for the vision is yet for many days."*

If Satan could block Paul, then how much more will he be able to block us from doing what we know to be right? It is a fact that if we expect success in our Christian lives, then we should also expect to hear some rumbling from Satan in the background trying to block us.

Our path to the Kingdom is fraught with many trials and temptations. We have never been told our path would be easy, but in fact, the very opposite is true. We are told to expect troubles of all kinds in this world.

When we conclude that whatever is hindering us is from Satan, then what can and what should we do? We should do as Paul did. We should continue on our path towards our calling in God as the Holy Spirit enables us, regardless of what Satan tries to do to derail us from our destination. To stop is to give in to Satan. To continue is to please God.

I believe that when the Devil is quiet and not causing us any trouble. Then this is probably a sign that we are not doing much to upset him. But when we are being slandered, and the world seems to hate us, and our names are mud to the rest of the world, then we must be doing something that upsets Satan.

We cannot do anything good and worthwhile to advance the gospel, for helping our fellow man. For doing good towards our fellow Christians, expecting no opposition from our enemy. So when we feel that hindrance from Satan, we must expect to have a fight on our hands, and then we will not be disappointed. If we go through a full year with no resistance from Satan, then he probably thought that we were not worth the effort and he would find someone else worth attacking.

It is much better to preach will all of our strength, soul and might the gospel of Jesus Christ. Then people of this world will put a fool's cap on our heads and try to make a laughingstock of us and ridicule us for what we believe in. But why should we let that worry us? Because we are not alarmed because Satan is trying to hinder us.

We are all aware of the fact that Satan is always on the lookout for people to draw away from God. It is his ambition to destroy everything that is of God.

> *1Pe_5:8 Be alert and of sober mind. Your enemy the devil prowls around like a roaring lion looking for someone to devour.*

If there is one lesson to learn from this post, then this is it. Satan is a past master at using people and circumstances to alter the path God has set out for you. John Calvin said it very well when he said. "Whenever the ungodly cause us trouble, they are fighting under the banner of Satan, and are his instruments for harassing us."

Naturally, these people will not realise they are under Satan's banner, but that does not change the fact that they are.

There will be times in your life when you may feel compelled to speak to someone. To do a certain service for a friend or neighbour. But you do not do it. This may just be Satan's way of obstructing you. This is when you must learn to resist Satan.

After Jesus was baptised by John The Baptist, he spent 40 days out in the wilderness and was tempted many times by Satan. Jesus rebuked him every time with a passage from scripture, from what we call the old testament. The new testament had not been written by this time.

Satan knew exactly who Jesus was and also knew if he could get Jesus to worship him instead of God. Then he would have had a major victory over God. He failed in all of his endeavours. But so great was his pride. He actually thought he could change the course of God's plans.

Mar_1:13 and he was in the wilderness for forty days, being tempted by Satan. He was with the wild animals, and angels attended him.

The vast majority of Christians who actually believe in Satan never consider he may have access to Heaven. When you read the book of Job, you will see he can come before God.

Job 1:6 Now on the day when God's sons came to present themselves before Yahweh, Satan also came among them.

Job 1:7 Yahweh said to Satan, "Where have you come from?" Then Satan answered Yahweh, and said, "From going back and forth in the earth, and from walking up and down in it."

But there is a time still to come when he can no longer move between Earth and Heaven. He will be cast out of Heaven permanently and he will come down to Earth with great wrath. He will seek anyone he can hinder from doing God's will. We see in verse nine below he is described as "the deceiver of the entire world."

Rev 12:7 There was war in the sky. Michael and his angels made war on the dragon. The dragon and his angels made war.

Rev 12:8 They didn't prevail, neither was a place found for them any more in heaven.

Rev 12:9 The great dragon was thrown down, the old serpent, he who is called the devil and Satan, the deceiver of the whole world. He was thrown down to the earth, and his angels were thrown down with him.

Rev 12:10 I heard a loud voice in heaven, saying, "Now the salvation, the power, and the Kingdom of our God, and the authority of his Christ has come; for the accuser of our brothers has been thrown down, who accuses them before our God day and night.

Rev 12:11 They overcame him because of the Lamb's blood, and because of the word of their testimony. They didn't love their life, even to death.

Rev 12:12 Therefore rejoice, heavens, and you who dwell in them. Woe to the earth and to the sea, because the devil has gone down to you, having great wrath, knowing that he has but a short time."

Again, in Rev 20:2, Satan is portrayed as he who "deceived the whole inhabited earth."

Rev_20:2 He seized the dragon, the old serpent, which is the devil and Satan, who deceives the whole inhabited earth, and bound him for a thousand years,

Then comes some sound advice from Jesus in Mat 24:4.

Mat_24:4 Jesus answered them, "Be careful that no one leads you astray.

Those who will lead you astray are anyone who will try to divert you away from the will of God. When you know you should do good for someone, but decline for any reason. This is when you are being led astray.

Christians should always remember, spiritual warfare, angels, and Satan are very real. Satan is the sworn enemy of our saviour and his greatest purpose is to turn people away from Christ through his lies and deceit. It is therefore essential that

Christians remember this is a reality. To believe otherwise is just a recipe for spiritual disaster.

As we read in one John 5:18, no one can snatch us out of Christ's hands. But this does not stop him from trying to cause division among believers to render them in effective in their testimony about Jesus. This is just one reason we are called to "resist the devil". No matter what happens, we must stand firm and oppose the adversary of God's people.

We find that submitting to God and resisting the devil are the same thing. One commentator put it very well when he said, "submission to God is itself an act of resistance to the devil. As people align their lives with God, the result becomes growing resistance to the temptations of the devil and he loses any foothold and must flee". One of the most important things for us to remember is that we must submit our lives to God if we are to resist Satan. It would be arrogant to think otherwise.

After James had commanded us to resist the devil, he tells us we should "draw near to God, and he will drawn near to you".This is the only, and sure way to resist the devil.

When Jesus Christ returns in all power and glory at the end of this age, we see Satan's future. In the three verses below, we see Our Lord as being triumphant and Satan as being conquered.

> *Rev 20:1 I saw an angel coming down out of heaven, having the key of the abyss and a great chain in his hand.*

> *Rev 20:2 He seized the dragon, the old serpent, which is the devil and Satan, who deceives the whole inhabited earth, and bound him for a thousand years,*

> *Rev 20:3 and cast him into the abyss, and shut it, and sealed it over him, that he should deceive the nations no more, until the thousand years were finished. After this, he must be freed for a short time.*

We must always remember this and never give in to the influence of Satan.

Chapter 17 - The Good News

I could not possibly end the book here without some encouraging words from the bible. Satan has great power and is using it to influence us all away from God. He may be known as the prince of this world, but Jesus Christ is "THE KING OF KINGS AND THE LORD OF LORDS". He has the ultimate power in the universe.

There is a time coming, and I believe it will be soon, when Satan will be confined and will no longer be able to influence us and lead us away from God. The evidence of this is in rev 20:1-3

Rev 20:1 And I saw an angel come down from heaven, having the key of the bottomless pit and a great chain in his hand.

Rev 20:2 And he laid hold on the dragon, that old serpent, which is the Devil, and Satan, and bound him a thousand years,

Rev 20:3 And cast him into the bottomless pit, and shut him up, and set a seal upon him, that he should deceive the nations no more, till the thousand years should be fulfilled: and after that he must be loosed a little season.

We know from the book of Jeremiah that God has good plans for us as we see in.

Jer 29:11 For I know the thoughts that I think toward you, saith the LORD, thoughts of peace, and not of evil, to give you an expected end.

Jer 29:12 Then shall ye call upon me, and ye shall go and pray unto me, and I will hearken unto you.

Jer 29:13 And ye shall seek me, and find me, when ye shall search for me with all your heart.

Heb 2:14 Forasmuch then as the children are partakers of flesh and blood, he also himself likewise took part of the same; that through death he might destroy him that had the power of death, that is, the devil;

Heb 2:15 And deliver them who through fear of death were all their lifetime subject to bondage.

1Co 15:51 Behold, I shew you a mystery; We shall not all sleep, but we shall all be changed,

1Co 15:52 In a moment, in the twinkling of an eye, at the last trump: for the trumpet shall sound, and the dead shall be raised incorruptible, and we shall be changed.

1Co 15:53 For this corruptible must put on incorruption, and this mortal *must* put on immortality.

1Co 15:54 So when this corruptible shall have put on incorruption, and this mortal shall have put on immortality, then shall be brought to pass the saying that is written, Death is swallowed up in victory.

1Co 15:55 O death, where *is* thy sting? O grave, where *is* thy victory?

1Co 15:56 The sting of death *is* sin; and the strength of sin *is* the law.

1Co 15:57 But thanks *be* to God, which giveth us the victory through our Lord Jesus Christ.

1Co 15:58 Therefore, my beloved brethren, be ye stedfast, unmoveable, always abounding in the work of the Lord, forasmuch as ye know that your labour is not in vain in the Lord.

Chapter 18 - Conclusion

Satan is referred to in the Bible as the "Prince of the Earth" and also as "the prince of the power of the air". He has much power here on the Earth. But remember, Jesus Christ is "THE KING OF kings and THE LORD OF lords."

Therefore, he trumps Satan in all things. He is the ultimate power and authority. And when he returns, which will be soon, Satan will be bound and put into a pit where he can no longer influence anyone.

So, put your faith in Jesus Christ who is "forever". Resist Satan, who is temporary.

Deu 4:29 But if from thence thou shalt seek the LORD thy God, thou shalt find him, if thou seek him with all thy heart and with all thy soul.

Deu 4:30 When thou art in tribulation, and all these things are come upon thee, even in the latter days, if thou turn to the LORD thy God, and shalt be obedient unto his voice;

Deu 4:31 (For the LORD thy God is a merciful God;) he will not forsake thee, neither destroy thee, nor forget the covenant of thy fathers which he sware unto them.

The Bible says that "the whole world is under the control of the evil one" (1 John 5:19[1]), and we must "be self-controlled and alert. Your enemy the devil prowls around like a roaring lion looking for someone to devour" (1 Peter 5:8[2]). Yet Christians have a great hope, for Jesus Christ (John 16:33[3]) and our faith in Him

---

1. https://www.bibleref.com/1-John/5/1-John-5-19.html

2. https://www.bibleref.com/1-Peter/5/1-Peter-5-8.html

3. https://www.bibleref.com/John/16/John-16-33.html

(1 John 5:4[4]) have overcome Satan's evil. "The one who is in you is greater than the one who is in the world" (1 John 4:4[5]).

---

4. https://www.bibleref.com/1-John/5/1-John-5-4.html

5. https://www.bibleref.com/1-John/4/1-John-4-4.html

About The Author

Leslie Rendell worked most of his life in an agricultural support industry, mostly in the supply of spare parts for machinery. Since his retirement in 2014 he has dedicated much of his time to bible study and writing books as he comes to understand biblical topics.

He understands the bible is a very complex book, and one that is easy to misinterpret and believes this is one of the main reasons why there are so many different version of the bible and different religions around the world.

What he writes is his own interpretation of God's holy scriptures. He studies the thoughts of other writers to try to see things from their point of view, but always comes back to the bible as the final authority on any topic. His main aim in writing, is to give anyone who is seeking the truth from God's words a starting point in their own research.

Leslie's other interest are photography, and his growing family.

Don't miss out!

Visit the website below and you can sign up to receive emails whenever Leslie Rendell publishes a new book. There's no charge and no obligation.

https://books2read.com/r/B-A-VDUV-WHNZC

BOOKS 2 READ

Connecting independent readers to independent writers.

Also by Leslie Rendell

Bible Studies
Three Days and Three Nights
According To Your Faith
Do Not Conform
How Long Was Jesus Christ in the Tomb
The Law of Moses
Abraham, Jesus and the Cross
Do We Have Immortal Souls
Be Holy
Is Being Fearful A Sin Against God
Mockers and the Return of Jesus Christ
Teachers During The Tribulation
Tearing of The Curtain in The Temple
The Thief On The Cross Alongside Jesus Christ
What Is The Rapture
The Imminence of the Rapture is a False Teaching.
Why The Pre-Tribulation Rapture Theory Is False
Are You Hindered By Satan
Satan is Targeting Man's Free Will
Why Is There So Much Suffering In Our World
The Sign of Jonah
Evil Is The Rejection Of God
Satan, Spirit Being With Many Names
Only One Sign
The Lord's Passover
The Resurrection of Jesus Christ